FROM CRISIS TO CALM

A PATIENT ADVOCATE'S TAKE ON HEALTHCARE COORDINATION

NICOLE CHRISTENSEN

RED PENGUIN Books

Thank you

The Greene Gang—"I'm everything I am because you loved me."
It is through our family's crisis, loss, love, faith and support that I
am a Patient Advocate (and everything I am).

My children Ian and Blaise, my loves; always making me proud
and cheering me on.

My husband, Christian, our captain even through the storms.

My friends and family (you know who you are) always believing
in a dreamer.

All my many healthcare colleagues who are dedicated to
utilizing their expertise and experience to provide quality and
compassionate care.

All the caregivers—Yes, YOU—Without your care none of us
would be here. We owe you our lives.

CONTENTS

DISCLAIMER

Neither this book nor the author is a health care provider, and this book does **not** provide medical advice, diagnosis, prescriptions and/or treatments, legal advice, psychological or psychiatric care or counseling, or financial, accounting or insurance counseling.

Always seek medical advice from one or more duly licensed physicians or health care professionals before making any decision related to health care. You should always seek legal advice from one or more duly licensed attorneys before making any decision related to legal matters.

INTRODUCTION

" *There are only four kinds of people in the world: those who have been **caregivers**, those who are currently **caregivers**, those who will be **caregivers**, and those who will need **caregivers**.*

~*Rosalynn Carter*

Many of us are all four of these kinds of people at the same time! Caregiving is exhausting, joyful, rewarding, life-giving and life-stripping work. Caregiving is the work of superheroes! You are part of this illustrious club, so give a nod to your fellow comrades (you will need each other) and fasten your invisible cape.

So here are the facts: "Family caregivers are more likely to experience negative health effects like anxiety, depression and chronic disease . . . One study found that long-term caregivers have disrupted immune systems even three years after their caregiving roles have ended." (*The study was led by Dr. Janice Kiecolt-Glaser at Oho State University in* 2003.) So caregivers need help. Let's start first by identifying a caregiver. YOU are a CAREGIVER.

WHAT DOES IT MEAN TO BE A CAREGIVER?

There is not one kind of caregiver. Caregiving can include:

- Caring for children
- Caring for an adult
- Taking someone to doctor appointments to make sure they have a second pair of ears
- Bringing food or supplies to a friend or neighbor who needs some help
- Checking in on parents who live across the country
- Helping an aunt pay her bills and get the right insurance
- Research and set up care in the home for a loved one who wants to remain independent at home
- Accompanying someone you care about to their chemo appointments
- Sitting bedside at the hospital
- You can have a big family who all help out with the different needs of your parents
- You can have a big family (or no family) but YOU are the only one that helps with care.

- Worrying about a loved one, neighbor or friend but not knowing how to assist them
- Provide emotional support for a loved one
- Feeling as if you have to be your own caregiver
- Caring for a loved one living in your home.

So what is a Patient Advocate and how can they help a super-hero like yourself? As a private professional Patient Advocate and caregiver myself, I have seen and navigated many of the situations you have and will face. We do not replace you as a friend or loved one (no one can do that); we help you navigate these complicated systems of healthcare so the path can be easier for you and your loved ones. We know you want the best care for your loved one's unique needs.

This book is a tool to help you access those options best for you so you can focus more on being that special someone and taking care of everyone and everything else in your life, including family members and career. This book will help you ask the right questions and act on the information to get the best care.

WHO NEEDS PATIENT ADVOCACY AND CARE COORDINATION?

Answer: Patients! And especially those over 65 or caring for loved ones over 65.

Here are some noteworthy statistics you should know as a patient and caregiver.

Preventable Medical Error in hospitals in is the 3rd Leading Cause of Death in the US (*Published May 3, 2016 in "The BMJ" citing an 8-year study at Johns Hopkins University.*)

- 80,000 deaths annually are a result of diagnosis errors

- 90,000 deaths occur annually due to hospital infections

- 1.5 million medication errors occur annually

- Every 11 seconds an older adult is treated in the emergency room for a fall; every 19 minutes an older adult dies from a fall. (*Study by the U.S. Centers for Disease Control and Prevention, cited by the National Council on Aging.*)

Nearly half of US adults are Health illiterate. This means they do not have the capacity to obtain, process, and understand basic health information and services needed to make appropriate health decisions. And those adults **65+ have the lowest health literacy.** (*https://health.gov/communication/literacy/issuebrief*)

- 49% of the workforce expects to be providing eldercare in the next 5 years (42% have already provided eldercare in the past 5 years) (*AARP Public Policy Institute*)

- 2 out of 3 workers in the US between the ages of 45 and 74 are caregiving for an aging or other adult relative. (*National Alliance for Caregiving*)

- Currently 5.9 million Americans have Alzheimer's Disease. That number is expected to be nearly 14 million by 2050. (*Alzheimer's Association*)

These numbers illustrate that "You are Not Alone."

Patient Advocates and Care Coordinators allow loved ones to

be loved ones (and stay employed and care for other members of their families). We Get Healthcare DONE.

Patient Advocates can provide a myriad of services and often have different specialties. For example, they can specialize in specific illness or age groups. Here is a brief overview of the work of Patient Advocates and Care Coordinators like myself and Care Answered staff.

I feel Patient Advocacy and Care Coordination is often required at the toughest times of a patient's journey, and when proper care and information can be the most difficult to achieve. I call this "transition periods."

DOCTOR'S APPOINTMENT

• Your spouse has a doctor's appointment and comes back with less information than when she/he left for the appointment. Apparently the doctor ordered tests, but what they are for and what those tests could tell you is utterly unclear. You then try to call the doctor's office but can't get through. You and your spouse are now stressed, nervous, and still not informed. Patient Advocates will go to the doctor appointments with you. They have already truly listened to the concerns of both you and your spouse. The Patient Advocate is prepared with questions to ask and will write down the answers to get you all the information you need to know.

DIAGNOSIS

• You receive a diagnosis and don't know quite how to deal with that information. The sooner you get a Patient Advocate the more they can do for you. Again, the Patient Advocate will already have gone over your history and concerns about your health ahead of time. They will still be asking the questions when you and your loved one's heads may be fogged by the emotion of the situation. They will be writing down the information and making sure you understand all of it. They are also going to schedule you a second, and perhaps third opinion, and be there for you for those appointments, too.

BEING HEARD

• The clinician doesn't seem to be listening to you and you are about to convince yourself that s/he knows what they are doing and be quiet and not speak up. This is the case more often than not. You may also tell yourself you will look online rather than asking the professional in front of you who has details of your specific case. What happens is that you go home and then google yourself into a frenzy. You find out that your concerns could be both valid and/or nothing to worry about. The outcome is more stressful. You have less ability to move in a direction to where your questions get answered or your concerns addressed. Patient Advocates speak up when you find it difficult to do yourself or for your loved one. And the sooner you hire a Patient Advocate the better so that you don't end up in a crisis.

SURGERY?

• You are determining whether or not to have surgery. This is similar to the doctor office advocacy. You need to make sure that all of your health concerns have been both vocalized and understood by the clinician involved. You must make sure that all appropriate tests, to rule out or to determine the diagnosis, have been done to properly discern if surgery is necessary for YOU. Patient Advocates are there to make sure those questions are asked, answered and fully understood by YOU. In addition where you have the surgery, expectations of recovery, and health care proxy will be fully addressed.

INSURANCE

• You believe that if one doctor who is on your insurance orders tests for you, suggests other specialists for you to see, hospitals to go to etc., that all of these must be covered under your insurance. Insurance can get tricky and may need to be looked at in advance of all of these. You have heard the story of the "routine test" that is unexpectedly not covered by your insurance and then comes the bill for thousands of dollars. Patient Advocates can help ensure that there are no surprise bills, and be the liaison between you and your insurance company.

TESTS, TREATMENTS AND PREP, OH MY?!

• You don't even know where to begin to prepare for the therapies and treatment that your clinician has set up. Perhaps you have had the experience of having a treatment for the condition scheduled and then realize on the day of treatment that you were not prepared for this! Perhaps you didn't ask questions regarding how patients generally feel or what foods to eat, or how long the reactions of the treatment may last. Or maybe you did know the possibilities, but felt that you were not going to be the person on the other end of that spectrum. So, now you have nothing in place. A Patient Advocate will help put things in order "in case" you end up with the more challenging reaction that temporarily impacts your general way of living. And if you do not need all the "in case" provisions, that is great, however, at least it is not what you have to spend your energy on when all of the focus should be on healing.

HOSPITAL DISCHARGE

• You are being discharged from the hospital. Yay! But you do not want to be someone who is in no way prepared to care for themselves and end up back in the hospital. *What do I need to know?* First know that Discharge planning begins at admission. Yes, you read that correctly—*admission.* The whole reason to go to the hospital is to get better, so the discharge plan, although evolving as you are treated at the hospital, begins right away. And this is definitely one of those areas where lack of or unclear information can be devastating. You can find yourself at home with none of the necessary care in place making you more likely to end up back in the hospital, or worse. Or you can end up in a physical rehabilitation facility, which is way too far from any loved ones and with no equipment available to help you recover.

A Patient Advocate makes sure the discharge plans are developed, clear to the patient and their caregivers and they set up the appropriate care for the patient's unique needs. They can keep you out of the hospital and recovering quicker.

USING THAT LONG-TERM CARE POLICY

• It is now time to activate that Long-Term Care Policy that your dad paid into for all these years. Unfortunately, many of us know that buying insurance is the easy part but making them pay for the services you need is eminently more difficult. Patient Advocates review the policy for you (sometimes helping you get a copy of it from the insurance company). And Patient Advocates effectively communicate with the insurance company, doctors, and any other relevant health entity to ensure you have documented proof to submit so that you get the claim in and get the care needs paid.

DECLINE IN HEALTH

• You notice that Aunt Sally's health is deteriorating but don't know what to do. This often happens at holidays when there are enough people witnessing the deterioration that it can not be rationalized away. (I recommend doing something before you get a consensus, as the sooner someone gets help the better the outcome can be.) A Patient Advocate can suggest doctors, specialists, and transportation, as well as review medications and advocate at the doctor's appointments. In addition, the Patient Advocate can be the liaison between the entire care team, including the family and pharmacist, so nothing falls through the cracks.

HOME OR NURSING HOME?

• Dad needs care at home. We promised him that we would not send him to a nursing home. How do we do this? Patient Advocates will review the options available so that it is clear how to get his wishes met in the best way possible.

GETTING RESULTS

• We are not getting answers back after the vital test and the stress is killing us. A Patient Advocate will liaison for you after the tests, as well as set up expectations with the lab and doctors before the tests, so that you are less likely to find yourself waiting apprehensively.

• They can't do the test for another two weeks and we may all pass out if we don't know more, sooner. A Patient Advocate will coordinate with your doctors, insurance and testing sites to exhaust the possibilities of where, when, and how to get the tests done effectively.

OVERWHELMED; HELP!

• We have children of our own and work full time. We need help navigating the care system so we can make sure the best care is in place for our parents. This is another case where a Patient Advocate and Care Coordinator can bring peace of mind while accessing your loved ones' best care. This can include looking outside the box to find options of therapies and activities that can increase quality of life as well.

> ❝ *Jane's family called me when she was transferred from the hospital to the skilled nursing facility for physical rehabilitation. This was the 3rd time this had happened in the last five months. Jane's physical weakness and recurring bronchitis is what kept bringing her back to the hospital. Every time she was discharged from the hospital, fainting spells occurred and this time she fell and fractured her collar bone. So in an effort to end this vicious cycle of hospital, rehab, home repeat, as well as the emotional trauma of continually being in hospital settings and the delirium that comes with it, Jane and her family called me in to be her Patient Advocate. This is not an uncommon case. Often a hospital needs to discharge patients after there is no "medical need" for them to be in the hospital, yet the diagnosis may not be clear to the patient. Then the patient is discharged to a skilled nursing facility for physical and occupational rehabilitation. However, the rehabilitation facility is focusing on the rehab and potentially not the diagnosis or prescribed medications. This same patient may not progress well in rehab because they did not receive the medications they truly need and were prescribed, in addition the root cause of the illness requiring them*

to need rehab has not been addressed. In this case, Jane was weak and she broke her collarbone so she was getting rehab to get her walking assisted, but the medications she needed to prevent the fainting were not given (the rehab ordered a lower cost medication that was not correct for her condition) and the sporadic weakness was not addressed.

After working with Jane, her community clinicians, family, rehab team, as well as reviewing hospital discharge plans, we were able to get her to specialist appointments (even while in rehab), schedule appropriate testing, get second opinions, obtain an accurate diagnosis, and receive appropriate medications for all her conditions. In this way, the cycle of no answers ended and knowledge and treatment choices could begin.

*To Err is Human;Building a Safer Healthcare System

https://news.gallup.com/poll/148670/caregiving-costs-economy-billion-lost-productivity.aspx

https://www.aarp.org/content/dam/aarp/ppi/2015/caregiving-in-the-united-states-2015-report-revised.pdf

https://health.gov/communication/literacy/issuebrief/

2

YOU GOT THIS: PLANNING

My 75 year old Mom is spry and active and lives on her own. She has had health concerns in the past but she is a fighter and she is doing great. My spouse and I work and have children. We live nearby Mom and she will even babysit for date night.

Are You Ready? You Got This! Ready for what, you ask? The truth is, this is the story from many Care Answered clients. We cannot predict what happens in our lives but we can be better prepared so that we can put the best care in place. Here is a real life scenario:

Mom was considered the "mayor" of her building. She was still an active real estate agent. Everyone knows her and she takes her two-mile walk every morning. Two weeks ago she slipped and fell and we thought nothing of it. She was not hurt; she just lost her footing. The other day she fell outside and was rushed to the hospital. It looked really bad. The doctors say she needs surgery and they are asking us who is the health care proxy and what does she want if she becomes incapacitated. I can't think straight and I don't know the answer. She was so healthy; we never talked about her wishes. I don't know what to do!

So what do you need to prepare? Here are some things that should be discussed ideally when we are healthy and before any crisis.

First here are some common terms to familiarize yourself with when planning for long term needs:

- **DNR**—Do Not Resuscitate
- **Resuscitate**—the action or process of reviving someone from unconsciousness or apparent death.
- **DNI**—Do Not Intubate
- **Intubate**—To put a tube in, commonly used to refer to the insertion of a breathing tube into the trachea for mechanical ventilation

HOW TO PREPARE BEFORE ANYTHING HAPPENS:

- Family discussion on what Mom wants (i.e., what

happens if she can't live alone anymore, DNR or not, DNI or not)

- Financial discussion about what can Mom afford if/when she needs additional help at home or outside of the home

- Mom should meet with an Elder Law attorney to have a healthcare proxy and Power of Attorney and much more in place. Someone needs to be able to make financial and health decisions on her behalf if she is incapacitated.

The selected healthcare proxy needs to have all medical records on hand including a list of diagnoses, medications (doses, what they are for, when they are taken), and a list of doctors. This needs to be updated and dated as often as necessary.

- Someone should be attending doctor appointments with Mom to advocate and have a second set of ears.

- Encourage Mom to go to a Primary Care Physician (PCP) that she trusts so that she will feel comfortable relaying all of her health concerns. If appropriate, I recommend people 70 years of age and older to see a Geriatric doctor, as they are specialists for those in that age group, for just the same reason most children see a Pediatrician.

Let's take a step back and figure out how you can really be in "You Got This" status. When you or a loved one becomes ill, or health is deteriorating, is not the time when you want to be in the "coulda, woulda, shoulda" state of mind. It is stressful, energy-draining, and heart-wrenching; so let's avoid heaping anymore on top of that. **Here are some steps to take now:**

1. Discuss with your loved ones what kind of care you may want to receive if you were faced with a catastrophic health event and could not speak for yourself. This does not need to be morbid or even particularly uncomfortable. I like to use holidays, like Thanksgiving, Christmas, Passover or April 16th for these kinds of discussions. Take advantage of these are times when loved ones are more likely gathered so it can be a family/friend tradition and then "pass the gravy". April 16th however, is a date you can put on your calendar—it is National Healthcare Decisions Day. It falls just after the traditional "tax day". As we all know the two things we can be certain of are death and taxes. We may not like to talk about paying our taxes but most of us do so at least once a year. So, why would your own health choices not be as important as taxes?

HOW DO YOU TALK ABOUT HEALTHCARE DECISIONS?

Once you have selected your healthcare agent or proxy, be sure to inform that person about his or her role, and let him or her know about your wishes should an illness or injury leave you unable to make your own healthcare decisions.

It's not taboo. Just bring it up at the dinner table. Try these opening lines:

> *"My faith is important to me and I don't want to have . . ."*
> *"I'm allergic to . . . Please make sure that I don't receive that medicine."*

Talk about what you value, and be as specific as you can. You might say:

> *"I don't want to ever be sustained by machines," or "I have to be able to live independently," or "There are new health findings every day. I would like to be kept alive until they find a cure."*

There are even suggestions on how to start this conversation to make it easier. Check out: http://theconversationproject.org/wp-content/uploads/2017/02/ConversationProject-ConvoStarterKit-English.pdf

Remember this is an ongoing conversation, not a one-and-done conversation, especially with your selected health care proxy/agent.

2. Health Care Proxy/Health Care Agent—This is the person you select to make these healthcare decisions for you in case you are incapacitated. How do I pick this person? This is someone you trust who can make sure your health care wishes for yourself are carried out. This is not necessarily the one who loves you most, or the child who could use some more responsibility or even the child who is so responsible when it comes to money but lives in another country for the foreseeable future. It is a person who is generally a close family member or friend who knows your general wishes in regard to health measures, and is able make sure they are carried out. The discussion with your healthcare proxy can, and should be, ongoing.

You cannot imagine every possible scenario, however if your healthcare proxy understands your values and knows the types of life-sustaining treatments that you would want, as well as those interventions that you would not want, she/he will feel confident that they are following **your wishes** rather than having to decide your fate on their own. The reason this is an ongoing discussion is because your thoughts may change as you age, your health changes, the healthcare system changes, science advances, religious beliefs evolve, etc.

Perhaps this description will help bring it to light. Think of making a Will. You have a puppy and you love him! In making your will, you want to make sure if anything should happen to you, the puppy is well cared for. You have one loving, wonderful daughter halfway across the country who would do anything for you. However, she both hates dogs and is highly allergic to them. In addition, her five-year-old son (your grandson) is also highly allergic and asthmatic. You also have a best friend who rescues dogs, takes care of your puppy now when you go on vacation, and is a natural-born dog whisperer. So who would be the best "guardian" for your dog should you be unable to care for him?

The choice is yours but if you're willing to make a decision based on the best interest of Fido and your loved ones, you must at least put as much effort into your own healthcare decisions.

3. Will—I will (pun intended) make this brief. You know what it is and you know you need to get one done. First, if you are one of those people who thinks, "I'll be dead. Who cares?" You should think again. Yes, you will be dead, but I have seen families get absolutely decimated when loved ones do not have a will. I'm pretty sure that's not a legacy you want to leave. Secondly, if you have no one to whom you wish to leave anything but do have something to leave (house, car, money, jewelry, etc.) and want it to go to charity, it will not go to charity unless you specify in a Will. Lastly, NO ONE has ever died from making a Will. It has been on no death certificate ever. I have no horse in this race other than you. I do not draft wills but for your family's sake, get it done. And you will have such a sense of accomplishment when you do it.

4. Power of Attorney—Like a healthcare proxy, this gives a person you select the ability to make the financial decisions for you in case you become incapacitated. So this person is in charge of your money and your bills IF you become incapacitated. This person also has to be selected wisely. It is not a popularity contest. This person will have a lot of work to do if they are put to use. What often is not mentioned is that the Power of Attorney and the Healthcare Proxy often have to work in close conjunction. Healthcare costs money. You DON'T want your Power of Attorney unnecessarily pinching pennies while your healthcare proxy has no money for life-sustaining medications you would want. So again, the discussions on healthcare should be made with everyone, especially these two.

5. **Hire an Elder Law Attorney**—To get all this legal groundwork covered and put in a legal document.

Many people when they hear "elder law attorney" think:

1. I don't think I really need one; what are they for anyway?
2. An attorney costs too much money.
3. My cousin, sister, uncle, friend is an attorney, so they will help if I need it.

Sound familiar? Well it's time to re-evaluate.

Let's begin with "What is an elder law attorney?"

An elder law attorney specializes in, you guessed it, elder law. "Elder and Special Needs Law" are specialized areas of law that involve representing, counseling, and assisting seniors, people with disabilities, and their families in connection with a variety of legal issues, from estate planning to long-term care issues, with a primary emphasis on promoting the highest quality of life for the individuals. Typically, Elder and Special Needs Law attorneys address the client's perspective from a holistic viewpoint by addressing legal, medical, financial, social and family issues."—*National Academy of Elder Law Attorneys.* (NAELA)

This is a nice neat definition from NAELA. However, not only do you need to find an elder law attorney, you need to find a good one who actually does **"address the client's perspective from a holistic viewpoint."** They need to really know the many facets of elder law; law changes all the time so you need to make sure your attorney is keeping up and knows the ins and outs.

Yes, lawyers cost money. However, not putting things in place so that your needs can be addressed is much more costly and heartbreaking for your entire family. Commonly, we see elder law attorneys provide estate planning (so one's hard-earned money and assets are given and used as they wish), creating wills and power of attorney, as well as Medicaid planning and application processing. Unfortunately, those who wait until the crisis hits to seek legal help are faced with fewer options and may lack access to the care they truly need.

Here is what you need from an elder law attorney:

- Someone who will first listen to your individual situation.
- From this information (and potential paperwork), they lay out and explain a plan to protect your assets and promote your highest quality of life.
- They follow through with this plan and tie up any loose ends so that, in the event of a crisis, you don't need to worry about this aspect.
- They can refer you to a Healthcare Coordinator and/or Patient Advocate who can provide healthcare advocacy and navigate you through the system of care.

Tips to find a good elder law attorney for your needs:

- Do they offer presentations on elder law basics? Or free consultations? This is helpful because many people don't know how much an elder law attorney can help and this gives insight and shows they may know what's current in the industry.
- How long have they been practicing ELDER LAW? There are plenty of young, fairly new Elder Law attorneys who are great!—however make sure they have the exact experience needed. I suggest Elder Law attorneys who truly specialize in elder law. It's the old adage of "a jack of all trades and an expert at none."
- If you know some of your needs, ask the firm how

many similar type of cases they handle annually, and ask if there are general pitfalls with this kind of case.

- A referral from this Patient Advocate or a friend who has used the attorney (for similar needs) with great success is also great.
- Do your homework. Just because the nursing home, long-term care facility or other healthcare entity suggests a lawyer does not necessarily mean they are good. They may even work for the facility or they may have just dropped off their business card with them.

5. MOLST/POLST—Have you heard of it? If not, you are not alone. MOLST (Medical Orders for Life Sustaining Treatment) or POLST (Physician Orders for Life Sustaining Treatment) are forms that can be very helpful for everyone who may have a prognosis of a year or so to live. No, this is not too morbid to discuss. As a Patient Advocate, I have found this tool to be most helpful and everyone needs to understand that the prognosis statement is not set in stone. Patients and families find filling out the forms useful because it forces you to have the conversations, including advising on one's wishes if illness or injury leaves you incapacitated, with one's loved ones AND your doctor. Notice the words "Medically ordered"—you need to complete this when you are cognitively able and your doctor is witness to it. A MOLST, unlike a DNR or DNI, follows you whether you are in the hospital in a different state, a nursing home, rehab or home. And because it is "medically ordered" there are less gray areas for medical professionals to disagree with the healthcare proxy or a living will.

The living will is a legal document. It is very useful in documenting necessary decisions made by the person and helps their healthcare proxy, but will generally not hold up in a medical situation. I believe the key to making the most of a MOLST is having a robust discussion on what you wish to do with the remainder of your life. Do you want to garden in your own garden forever? Do you want to travel to and with your family? Do you want to sail off into the sunset? Do you want to remain in your home or get care from a facility in your last days? Everyone is different, but this form can put more of these into action as you discuss with your doctor what would be needed for you medically to be able to do those quality of life things you wish to do.

6. Patient Advocate—Surprise! I suggest you also look into getting a private Patient Advocate! No, you are not surprised. Truly the right Patient Advocate can help you navigate all of these things. We can walk you through these planning discussions, help you locate an appropriate Elder Law Special Needs Attorney or Estate Planning Attorney, locate doctors and specialists, be there to help mediate family discussions regarding advanced directives and next steps, advocate at the doctor's appointment to ensure the clinician and patient are both being heard, and understood, and follow up steps can be taken, as well as liaising with insurance so it is clear what is and would be covered.

There is a great list of all the advanced planning steps that can really get you organized. *My End of Life Decision Guide Toolkit* put together by the not-for-profit Compassion and Choices. https://compassionandchoices.org/wp-content/up-loads/2018/09/My-End-of-Life-Decisions-Guide-Toolkit-FINAL-8-28-18.pdf

3

DOCTOR/CLINICIAN VISIT ADVOCACY

I t is time to go to the doctor, everyone's favorite thing to do! If you feel *This is certainly not my first visit to the doctor. What could I possibly need to know?* you are not alone. But you are probably wrong. Yep, I said it. So let me elaborate. If you are over the age of 40 you probably already have a different specialist that you visit regularly. Most of us had different doctors earlier than that. It feels like each body part has a different doctor associated with it, so it can be tricky to keep organized. Also a patient generally gets about 10-15 minutes per clinician. In addition, most people want to get out of the office as soon as possible, but a little bit of preparation to use your time wisely can go a long way. The best way to get the most of your clinician appointment is to take some action. Here are some steps:

PREP FOR VISIT

Get a health notebook (there is one in the back of this book)— Utilize this notebook for only your health issues. You will want to date it, and if relevant put the time of day of anything you include in your health notebook. Place it in an easy-to-access place in your home. This is the kind of information you could jot down or place in that notebook:

- Date any new information regarding your health (i.e., new diagnosis, new doctor, etc.)

- Any type of changes after a new medication (good or bad)

- Anything that seems "off" mentally or physically and date it

- Symptoms you have been feeling and what you think they could be linked to (i.e., I have had three migraines in the last month, which is a lot more than usual. I think it is because of the change in season)

- List questions, concerns or clarification you want to gain from this visit. You should have this list in your health notebook so you can write down the response in the notebook. You can also provide a copy of this list to the clinician so they have it and know what they need to cover it in the visit. Please note that if your list of questions is 3 pages long indicate your most pressing concerns and schedule a follow up appointment if necessary. You may not get to all questions in one visit if the list is that lengthy.

MEDICATION LIST

The medication list should include **ALL** medications, prescribed, over-the-counter, supplements, and vitamins. This list should be on your person and brought to doctor visits to review with each doctor. In addition, the caregiver/healthcare proxy should have an updated medication list at all times as well. An example follows, with a blank medication tracker in the back of the book for your use.

Current Medications
(including prescribed, OTC, herbal . . .)

Medication	Dosage and Instruction	Reason	Comments (ie. who prescribed, time of day taken, affects of usage, food combinations, etc.)
i.e.Ezetimibe	10mg once per day taken in the evening with dinner	High cholesterol	Dr. Jones

SPEAK UP AT THE APPOINTMENT

You have your health notebook out and you have given your clinician the list of questions and concerns you had before the appointment began. Now you:

- Listen—Actively listen to the doctor so you are focused at that moment
- Talk Back—Reiterate what you heard the doctor state back to the doctor in your own words. If s/he says "yes, that's right" then you know you have understood the information correctly.
- Write down—Yes, write down what the doctor said immediately while it is fresh in your brain. You will not remember it, so now is the time to write it down.

ASK QUESTIONS—I CANNOT PREDICT ALL
QUESTIONS RELEVANT FOR EACH CIRCUMSTANCE,
BUT THE FOLLOWING ARE SO COMMON THAT
ANSWERS ARE NEEDED:

What is the test for?

How many times have you done this procedure?

When will I get the results?

Why do I need this treatment?

Are there any alternatives?

What are the possible complications?

Which hospital is best for my needs? (Which hospital has the lowest infection rate?)

How do you spell the name of that drug?

. . .

Are there any side effects?

Will this medicine interact with medicines that I'm already taking?

Is there anything the doctor said that you did not fully understand? If so, ASK NOW. By reiterating what the doctor says both s/he and you will know if you truly understood. At the very least please ask the ASK ME 3 (National Safety Foundation) questions:

What is my main problem?

What do I need to do?

Why is it important to me?

Here is an example as to why these questions are so useful:

Dad goes into the doctor's office. You and Dad have articulated symptoms to your doctor. The doctor says a lot of things including a possible diagnosis and tests that are needed. These questions help to break it down.

What is Dad's main problem?

The doctor states: "He could have congestive heart failure and that means . . . "

What do we need to do?

The doctor states: "The next step is to have this test to determine if congestive heart failure is indeed the correct diagnosis. In the meantime, take these medications to relieve these symptoms."

Why is it important to us?

The doctor states: "Congestive heart failure undiagnosed or untreated can lead to heart failure and death. The symptoms you described could get significantly worse untreated. The test can confirm the diagnosis and get the treatment started to minimize symptoms and improve quality of life."

MEDICAL RECORDS

I advise you to have a copy of your medical records. In this age of technology, it should be easy for all your clinicians to access your medical records, but it is not. There is some research showing that the current most commonly used system of keeping medical records has played a part in additional medical errors. So let's leave as little up to chance as possible.

You may request medical records from all your clinicians. They can charge you up to 75 cents, per page currently. By law, your clinician is required to provide you with your medical records. Many of them may suggest you access "patient portals." Neither your medical records nor the portal will have all the information that your handy health notebook with your personal notes has in it. In your health notebook be sure to include all of the information to access each patient portal. I recommend that care-givers and patients regularly access your health portals. Ask your doctors if they have them. Many of the portals allow you to message your doctor and get a quick response. It's just another tool in accessing your best care (along with your trusty health notebook and copies of your past medical records, of course.) You do not have to have all your records for the last 40 years if they are not relevant. Ask for a copy of your records periodically so you are not asking for ten years of records during a crisis.

4

ADVOCACY AT THE HOSPITAL

Who's Who in the Hospital?

Let's speak about emergency situations first. This is a typical call:

> *"My Uncle John was feeling a little under the weather but was still doing his usual activities. Then he seemed to get a bit confused earlier today and, as the time progressed, has had trouble walking, and his confusion increased. I was trying to get him to the car to take him to the hospital but then realized we needed an ambulance. We are at the hospital and we can't seem to get any answers as to what happened."*

John was our client already. He hired us soon after being diagnosed with cancer to navigate and advocate for him through diagnosis and treatment. So we already knew his medical history. We came into the hospital after this call and brought his current list of medications and his medical history. When we arrived we quickly uncovered the hospital was going by incorrect information so we were able to rectify that immediately. John is allergic to shellfish so the contrast MRI they ordered could have killed him. The hospital nurse was under the impression that some of John's chemotherapy medications were taken orally and daily when in fact they were given via intravenous drip once every three weeks. The Patient Advocate acted as liaison to his primary care physician and all other specialists, as well as the hospital, so John was clear on the diagnosis, the cause, and the treatment. Care was coordinated and we followed him to short-term rehab and then back home with care until he was back to work. And finally, we stayed on to coordinate his care to resume treatment for cancer. His family was able to focus on quality time with him and their own careers and families. John was able to focus on healing and getting back to work.

No one wants to be in the hospital, yet, at least once in our lives, we find ourselves there. It is important for patients and their caregivers to know the players and who is who so that they can get their concerns addressed quickly and efficiently.

THE EMERGENCY ROOM

The primary job function of the ER doctors/clinicians is to resuscitate or stabilize patients and refer them to the appropriate medical departments. This is triage.

An ER staff person will ask why a patient is in the ER and inquire about relevant medical history and ask for a list of medications. Be prepared to tell the nurse this information and have it on paper as well. If you, even with no medical background, are concerned your loved one has had a stroke, heart attack or any life-threatening condition, say so immediately.

You cannot be blamed if you are wrong, and if you are right, appropriate tests or treatment may happen more quickly and make a real difference in the outcome.

Perhaps the staff at the hospital will ask you the same medical questions repeatedly. Although this can be frustrating, be prepared to answer. This is always my recommendation because I would rather them have accurate information than be guessing or somehow have misinformation due to human or technical error. And if you don't know the answer simply say you don't know.

ADMISSION INTO THE HOSPITAL

Admission is not the ER—a visit to the ER is not the same as being admitted to the hospital. Being admitted is when a patient has a serious issue that cannot be treated during an ER visit, or another location like an outpatient facility. If the patient has an illness or injury that cannot be treated quickly and is serious enough to warrant a hospital stay, the the ER doctor or a specialist will explain to the patient that their medical issue is serious and requires that the patient be admitted into the hospital. Generally, they will be moved to the part of the hospital that corresponds with the treatment or diagnosis the patient has. Here is a list of "who is who" once you are admitted.

Hospitalist

A Hospitalist is a physician whose only focus is the care of hospitalized patients. Once a person has become hospitalized, a Hospitalist acts as the patient's primary care physician in-house. The Hospitalist may be designated to one floor or unit of the hospital. Sometimes these doctors also have a private practice outside of the hospital, but many do not.

Nurse

Many of us know what a nurse does, however, there are nurses that serve different functions and have varying responsibilities and abilities to care for patients. There are many types of nurses such as Nurse Practitioners, Registered Nurses (RN), Licensed Practical Nurses (LPN), and Certified Nursing Assistants (CNA), to name a few. A Nurse Practitioner can offer care to a patient similarly to a doctor and can write prescriptions. Registered Nurses are the nurses that we typically think of when we think of nurses. RNs handle complicated medical responsibilities. An LPN has a license and generally reports to an RN, and has less direct medical care responsibilities. CNAs report to the RNs and LPNs, and they have the least medical responsibilities of this group. However, they may handle the most direct patient care. You may find all of these common types of nurses during a hospital stay.

Also, there is often a "Charge Nurse" who is in charge of all of the nurses on the unit of the hospital. There may also be a Nursing Supervisor who supervises the nurses for the entire Unit or floor. The patient's RN can let you know the list of medications they are currently giving, distribute medications, and can address your health concerns, or let you know who to contact. The RN can be a crucial point of contact for questions and concerns.

Specialists: (i.e. Orthopedic Doctor, Psychiatrists, Nephrologists)

Specialist doctors are doctors with a specialty and may be called on for your specific case. These doctors often have private practices outside the hospital as well. Although they have private practices, these Specialists you see in the hospital are allowed to be there because the hospital has granted them "privileges". A doctor with privileges at the hospital are allowed to operate, perform procedures, or admit patients to the hospital.

Primary Care Physician (PCP)

This is your doctor. This is the doctor you see for check-ups or if you have a health concern that you think may need treating. Your Primary Care Physician may be the doctor that recommends you go to the hospital based on your condition. Your Primary Care Physician may not have privileges at the hospital you go to—or any hospital—and will need to be updated on your situation.

Social Worker and Care/Case Managers

They are generally involved in preparing a safe discharge. The safe discharge allows a patient that has been admitted to the hospital to leave the hospital safely with care put in place at home or at a facility. Private Patient Advocates and Care/Case Managers often work closely with Social Workers at the hospital. They are often helpful in coordinating the healthcare, specialists and procedures while the patient is in the hospital as well.

PATIENT'S RIGHTS

This is in the hospital packet that you may have generally thrown out, misplaced and/or was never aware that you received. There is a document called "Patient Rights" (this is also provided in nursing homes). Always review it. Some of your questions can be answered right there. I find it can also give patients and caregivers more confidence when armed with the information that validates their questions. Here are your current patient rights in New York. You can look up the patient rights for other states online, as well.

As a patient in a hospital in New York State, you have the right, consistent with law, to:

1. Understand and use these rights. If for any reason you do not understand or you need help, the hospital MUST provide assistance, including an interpreter.
2. Receive treatment without discrimination as to race, color, religion, sex, national origin, disability, sexual orientation, source of payment, or age.
3. Receive considerate and respectful care in a clean and safe environment free of unnecessary restraints.
4. Receive emergency care if you need it.
5. Be informed of the name and position of the doctor who will be in charge of your care in the hospital.
6. Know the names, positions, and functions of any hospital staff involved in your care to refuse their treatment, examination or observation.
7. A nonsmoking environment.
8. Receive complete information about your diagnosis, treatment and prognosis.
9. Receive all the information that you need to give informed consent for any proposed procedure or treatment. This information shall include the possible risks and benefits of the procedure or treatment.

10. Receive all the information you need to give informed consent for an order not to resuscitate. You also have the right to designate an individual to give this consent for you if you are too ill to do so. If you would like additional information, please ask for a copy of the pamphlet "Deciding About Health Care—A Guide for Patients and Families."

11. Refuse Treatment and be told what effect this may have on your health.

12. Refuse to take part in research. In deciding whether or not to participate, you have the right to a full explanation.

13. Privacy while in the hospital and confidentiality of all information and records regarding your care.

14. Participate in all decisions about your treatment and discharge from the hospital. The hospital must provide you with a written discharge plan and a written description of how you can appeal your discharge.

15. Identify a caregiver who will be included in your discharge planning and sharing of post-discharge care information or instruction.

16. Review your medical record without charge. Obtain a copy of your medical record for which the hospital can charge a reasonable fee. You cannot be denied a copy solely because you cannot afford to pay.

17. Receive an itemized bill and explanation of all charges.

18. View a list of the hospital's standard charges for items and services and the health plans the hospital participates with.

19. You have a right to challenge an unexpected bill through the Independent Dispute Resolution process.

20. Complain without fear of reprisals about the care and services you are receiving and to have the hospital respond to you and, if you request it, a written response. If you are not satisfied with the hospital's response, you can complain to the New York State Health Department. The hospital must provide you with the State Health Department telephone number.

21. Authorize those family members and other adults who will be given priority to visit consistent with your ability to receive visitors.

22. Make known your wishes in regard to anatomical gifts. You may document your wishes to your health care proxy or on a donor card, available from the hospital.

INFECTIONS AND AVOIDING INFECTIONS

What is the leading prevention of infection? You guessed it! HAND WASHING. Make sure any staff or visitor who enters your room washes their hands or uses hand sanitizer. Make a sign if you need to, just make sure it happens. Do not forget you need to do it too, if you are able.

According to the CDC (Center for Disease Control) ***"On any given day, about one in 31 hospital patients has at least one healthcare-associated infection."*** So in addition to hand washing, the CDC also offers five other important suggestions to avoid infections in the hospital:

- Ask what they are going to do to prevent you from getting an infection. If you are having surgery, ask what they do to make sure the surgical site is clean and what you can you do before and after to help keep it clean.

- Ask about antibiotics. Many of us hear about infections that are "superbugs" or antibiotic-resistant. Ask if tests have been done to ensure you are taking the right antibiotics.

- Know the signs of a skin infection i.e., pain, redness or discharge at IV catheter or surgery site. This may be accompanied by a fever. Tell the doctor or nurse immediately if this happens.

- Tell them immediately if you have had 3 or more episodes of diarrhea in a 24-hour period, especially if you are on antibiotics.

- Get vaccinated for flu and other infections to avoid complications (always discuss this with healthcare provider.)

ADDRESSING CARE CONCERNS IN THE HOSPITAL

As a patient or caregiver, you should feel able—and really you should feel obligated—to state any concerns you may have while in the hospital. And you should not feel like you have to be a doctor to articulate your concerns. The sooner you speak up the better. Here is a somewhat easy acronym that can prove effective from the Agency of Healthcare Research and Quality: **CUS**

I am **Concerned**

I am **Uncomfortable**

I am **Scared/**there is a **Safety issue**

Tell a staff member in the hospital if you feel any of the three above issues, both as patient or caregiver. I would add to that "I need help." As a patient, feel free to state these concerns to any staff. However, if you are the caregiver, find the nurse assigned to the patient (see the previous section "Who's Who in the Hospital?") and tell the nurse. If you are not getting an adequate response from the assigned staff, move up the line until you get the attention of someone who can assist. You can explain more as you speak, or point or write (whatever capacity you have) now that you have their attention.

DISCHARGE PLANNING

Discharge planning begins at admission. That means the patient and team in the hospital should be working to get you out of the hospital as soon as you get there. As you probably agree after reading the hospital infection rates, it is not good for your health to stay in the hospital longer than necessary. However, a good discharge plan is essential, and this is discussed by the hospital team, as well as the patient and his or her family. The sooner these discussions occur, the easier it can be to put the plan into action.

I have had hospital patients call me to help them get out of the hospital. Take this client for example:

> *She was taken into the hospital with what now turns out to be sepsis. She does not like the food, she has things to do and wants to get out of the hospital TODAY! After some discussions with hospital nurses, the physical therapist and her primary care physician and family, it seems this could be an unsafe discharge. WHY?*

- Her muscles have been weakened by her condition and hospital stay. She is not yet able to walk on her own.

- She has nothing in place at home to help. (i.e. no walker or wheelchair).
- She is unable to get to the bathroom on her own.
- She does not have anyone in place at home to assist her.
- They have not yet discerned if the infection is indeed cleared.

As a Patient Advocate I was able to coordinate with the physical therapist, PCP, social worker, nurse supervisor, family members and home care agency and pharmacist to make sure the patient's concerns and needs were met. As a result of this patient advocacy, she was discharged from the hospital within 2 days and placed in a selected Skilled Nursing Rehabilitation Facility. Cultures came back indicating the infection was gone. A clear and aggressive plan, suitable for the patient, was made for physical and occupational therapy. This was put in place in order to potentially shorten her duration at the rehabilitation facility. I worked with the selected Certified Home Care Agency (CHA) to put in place a nurse and physical and occupational therapy in the home. Additionally medications were called in to her local pharmacist and discussed with the pharmacist. And lastly I made follow-up appointments with her PCP and Specialist and advocated at those appointments.

On the opposite side of the spectrum I have also had patients and their families calling me to advocate that they stay in the hospital.

One family called me after they came home from visiting with their Dad in the hospital. The hospital social worker called, letting them know their Dad would be discharged today back to his assisted living residence. The family was confused and very upset because they were just at the hospital. When they were at the hospital, Dad had not been able to get up on his own, and they got no answers regarding the cause of his confusion that led to hospitalization. This could also be an unsafe discharge. Why?

- The discharge plan was not explained well to the family, patient or assisted living facility. Due to the fact that the discharge plan was not explained no one could carry out whatever care instructions were necessary to create a safe discharge.

- A diagnosis was not given so there seemed to be no way to prevent this from occurring again and landing back in the hospital.

As a Patient Advocate, I was able to coordinate and liaison with the hospital staff including doctors, nurse, and social worker as well as the family, Assisted Living, and PCP. I asked questions like: "What could be causing this?", "Is it possible this is a result of medication and diet?", "What other tests could be performed?". This resulted in a halt to the hospital discharge and more tests to be done. In addition, the family requested individualized care while in the hospital for this patient. As the Patient Advocate, I researched, suggested and put in place, at the family's request, a home care aide who could be bedside with the patient in the hospital. Lastly, when diagnosis was able to be made, he was discharged 4 days later, with additional home care aides in place at the Assisted Living. In addition, the Patient Advocate put in place physical and occupational therapy, regular monitoring by his PCP at the Assisted Living facility, and follow-up with a Specialist outside the facility.

WHO IS WHO OUTSIDE THE HOSPITAL?

Hopefully, the "who's who in the hospital" section helped you better understand who to go to for different concerns in the hospital. However, there are others (clinicians, support, family) you should be speaking to who are potentially outside the hospital. Those people include:

Primary Care Physician (PCP)—Contact them and make sure that s/he is aware of the hospitalization and why they were hospitalized. Ask the PCP to contact the hospitalist or doctors within the hospital so that all your clinicians are on the same page in regard to your health and care.

Specialists the patient see outside the hospital— Contact these clinicians for the same reason as the primary care physician to make sure that s/he is aware of the hospitalization and why the patient was hospitalized. You want all your clinicians on the same page. Also a specialist could possibly add insight to the situation so that you, or the patient, receives the right care.

. . .

Family and friends who can help both in the hospital and after discharge into the community— Being hospitalized can be a very scary and lonely feeling. Visitors, calls, cards and other ways to show one cares can be very healing. In addition, I have never seen anyone who did not need some kind of help after hospitalization. So, as a caregiver, you can set up a visit calendar or create a meal calendar for family and friends after hospitalization. In addition, setting up follow-up visits to doctors or testing sites and picking up prescriptions can be a strenuous task for the patient. A loved one or the patient themselves can assign those tasks to another friend or loved one.

Medication Management—Dub someone willing, trusted, and able to be your Medication Manager. At discharge, a patient may be getting new medications in addition to old ones, they may now be discarding old medications, or it may be a confusing combination of both. At this point you already have their list of medications, dosages, what the medications treat, and when (i.e. AM or PM) you take them before the hospitalization. (You made sure this was done before you even got to this section of the book, right?! - see Chap 3) A Medication Manager was there at the discharge and should now have updated the old medication list and has dated it. This Medication Manager will discard from your home any medications no longer prescribed. They will make sure you have the correct dosage of all prescribed medications. The Medication Manager will also specifically let your pharmacist know all the medication changes. Both the patient and Medication Manager will have a copy of this updated list, as will your healthcare proxy, if that person is someone other than your Medication Manager. If appropriate this Medication Manager will acquire an appropriate pill box and help the patient fill the pill box.

Private Patient Advocate—The right Patient Advocates can help get this all done for you in and out of the hospital. Our experience and expertise can ease the journey for both the patient and caregiver allowing energy to heal and peace of mind.

5

NEEDING MORE CARE

There are a number of different ways to offer care. Many times there is a combination of services that may be the best fit. There is also quite a bit of confusion about the services that are out there and how/if they can fit into your loved one's budget. The best idea is to find a qualified Patient Advocate and/or Care Coordinator to navigate you through the maze, but let me demystify some of the options for you.

Independent senior living—These are communities generally for people 55 and over. They can be apartments, condominiums, single family homes or other private housing. Residents of Independent Senior Living communities DO NOT require skilled nursing assistance.

Please keep in mind there are those who are 55 and older living in this kind of Independent Senior Living community who also have home care aides or companion care in place to assist them. Generally, it is like living in your own home, just potentially surrounded by people of a similar age and easier access to activities and social engagements intended for the enjoyment of a population 55 and over.

Assisted Living—housing for elderly or disabled people that provides nursing care, housekeeping, and prepared meals as needed. Assisted living often gets confused with Skilled Nursing Facility (see following pages). They are not the same. In most cases, assisted living facilities have a "homey" setting, or in some cases a fancy hotel setting. People that utilize assisted living may just enjoy community dining rooms and group activities while their family has peace of mind, as there are some staff to check in on their loved ones. Others in assisted living may require medication reminders, benefit from a doctor being on-site periodically, and help from nurses during the day. Often times those who reside in an assisted living are able to ambulate (get around) on their own or with a walker or cane. Many Assisted Living sites do not have the capabilities to care for residents who are wheelchair or bed-bound. But keep in mind different Assisted Living sites may have very different offerings, so ask questions.

Following are tips and questions to ask when looking into assisted living. You will find a Health Notebook at the back of this book where you can record your answers.

What is the staff-to-resident ratio? (which staff is included in this ratio i.e. CNA, Nurses)

Do you have a designated area of living for those struggling with dementia? (sometimes referred to as memory units)

How often is a psychiatrist available to memory unit residents?

My loved one has dementia and I know there are many different stages and changes that can occur. Do you have experience with residents who get agitated? I know every resident can be different but can you give me an example of some practices you may employ?

What is the protocol for medication administration? Is it given within an hour for example or is it exactly on time?

How is the efficacy of medication monitored? (i.e. if a resident comes in for their usual medication but is unusually lethargic or agitated is there a protocol that takes place?)

.   .   .

What activities do you have for residents and how do you assist in the engagement of these activities?

How do you engage residents in activities when they are non-verbal? (Especially important if your loved one has dementia)

What activities are offered?

Do you allow outside and/or companion aides or Home Health Aide (HHA)? Keep in mind this will be an additional cost.

If we run out of money to pay for this assisted living, is there any way to stay here? If not, do you help us find appropriate placement?

If one becomes less ambulatory (i.e. needs a walker or wheel-chair to get around) will they be able to stay here?

HOME CARE

Medical Definition of **Home Health Aide (HHA)**: a trained and certified **health-care** worker who provides assistance to a patient in the **home** with personal **care** (i.e. hygiene and exercise) and light household duties (i.e. meal preparation) and who monitors the patient's condition—abbreviation **HHA**. HHAs are generally for someone residing at home. However, "home" could also be an independent senior living or assisted living. (Meriam-Webster.com)

Companion care - is primarily emotional support and companionship for seniors who are generally healthy and who want to remain independent at home. However, it can also include a range of non-medical services that help make a senior's life more manageable. Companion care is also generally used at home wherever that may be. Even some skilled nursing facilities will allow companion care to offer companionship to a resident. (Seniorliving.org/companioncare)

Following are tips and questions to ask when looking into home health aides or companion care. You will find a Health Notebook at the back of this book where you can record your answers.

1. Include your loved ones and primary care physician in the discussion about the need for home care and the type of care needed.

2. Make a list of daily activities in which you/your loved one may need assistance.

. . .

3. Determine what hours of the day and how many days a week you/your loved one needs care.

4. Prepare a list of medications (include supplements) that include when the medications are taken and what each medication is taken for. Keep in mind many home care agencies can't have their aides "administer" medications. This means they cannot take the medicines out of the bottle to give you but they can give reminders. (Always ask any care provider what they are able to do based on your list of daily activities in tip 2.)

5. Make a list of personality traits you/your loved one would find ideal—remember this person is in your home. Some examples: preference for someone chatty or quiet/reserved, is there a language in which you are more comfortable communicating, is there a preferred gender, is there a culture that you feel most comfortable around?

6. If you decide to find a home care agency or choose a home care provider privately, make sure a background check is done.

7. If possible, interview all perspective home care providers. Sometimes it is not possible to interview them in person or on the phone, so tips 1-6 are even more important to provide to the homecare provider.

. . .

8. Have a loved one or Patient Advocate stop by unannounced to make sure the homecare provider is meeting expectations.

Adult Day Care/Dementia Care—"Normally, adult day care is used to relieve the caregiver of his or her duties for the day while ensuring that the care recipient will still receive the proper care in a safe, friendly environment. These centers usually operate during normal business hours five days a week, and some centers also offer additional services during evenings and weekends. In general, there are three main types of adult day care centers: those that focus primarily on social interaction, those that provide medical care, and those dedicated to Alzheimer's care. Many of these facilities are affiliated with other organizations, including home care agencies, skilled nursing facilities, medical centers, or other senior service providers. The average participant in this type of program is a 76-year-old female who lives with a spouse, adult children, or other family or friends. About 50 percent of these individuals have some form of cognitive impairment and more than half require assistance with at least two daily living activities." Source: NationalCaregivers.org/whatisadultdaycare

Skilled Nursing Facility (SNF)/Rehabilitation- "Services generally available in a SNF: nursing care provided by registered professional nurses, bed and board, physical therapy, occupational therapy, speech therapy, social services, medications, supplies, equipment, and other services necessary to the health of the patient"—medicareadvocacy.org/nursing-home/skillednursingfacilitycare. This is commonly called a nursing home and may have a more hospital-like setting. Generally, doctors and specialist regularly visit the residents on site. Residents in nursing homes can be wheelchair or bed-bound and still receive care.

Following are tips and questions to ask when looking for SNF short-term rehab. You will find a Health Notebook at the back of this book where you can record your answers.

1. Visit potential sites and take note of smell, activity, interaction between patients and between staff and patients.

2. How many days do they offer each type of rehab (Physical Therapy (PT), Occupational Therapy (OT), and Speech Therapy)?

3. Obtain a list of medication from the hospital or home. Ask if the SNF is going to be able to access these medications so they will be available at upon arrival. This is especially important for prescriptions that are unusual or expensive or being used off-label (medication prescribed "off-label" is when a doctor prescribes medication that has been approved for different conditions than the condition being treated).

. . .

4. If your loved one is a fall risk, what precautions does the facility take to avoid falls?

5. What are visiting hours?

6. If your loved one has a condition that will impact their ability to be effective at rehab (i.e. pain, confusion, dizziness that may make it more challenging for them to cooperate with movement needed for therapy) make sure this is being treated at the hospital before they leave for rehab. Also bring it to the attention of the rehab facilityimmediately and ask if they have a specialist who can simultaneously treat it if needed.

7. If there are other medical concerns, make sure they have the equipment and personnel necessary (i.e. ventilator or dialysis) to treat that condition.

8. Review the PRI (Patient Review Instrument) to make sure it has accurate information, as this is what is sent to the potential rehabilitation sites. If something seems inaccurate, alert the nurse and ask them to make corrections before it is sent out.

. . .

9. Hire a Patient Advocate before hospital discharge so that you can be the loved one. Patient Advocates can utilize their experience and make this process easier for you and you can have peace of mind.

10. You want to articulate your loved ones baseline to the social worker, nurse and staff at the short-term rehab. "Baseline" means their skill level before entering the hospital that led to the need for rehab. Example is your loved one fell and broke their leg. Before they broke their leg they used a cane to walk. Therefore the baseline is they walked with a cane. So that would be the goal for rehab (barring any other circumstance).

11. Ask immediately when the care plan can be scheduled. The meeting brings all staff together (Social Worker, Nurse, PT, OT, Recreation, Speech etc. to discuss progress and next steps. The caregiver and patient are crucial in this plan. A Patient Advocate can represent the family/patient or join them in this meeting. They will make sure the care plan is clear and the steps toward reaching at least the baseline are clear to all.

12. Appealing the decision to discharge from a short-term rehabilitation facility is a common concern. Generally, a patient is discharged because there is no more progress being made in their physical, speech, and/or occupational therapies. Or, potentially the patient is not cooperating with the therapy. However,

a family may believe this is not valid. Having a Patient Advocate and Care Coordinator at the start can prevent this stress and doubt. This is very similar to hospital discharge. The key is to coordinate with the therapists, nurses, and doctors in the rehab as well as the PCP and specialists outside the rehab. There could be circumstances that prevent the patient from progressing that, if addressed, could expedite their movement toward their baseline (see Overwhelmed; Help in Chapter 1). You may win the appeal if you can prove that more therapy would indeed increase their progress.

Continuing Care Retirement Communities (CCRC) —"Part independent living, part assisted living and part skilled nursing home, CCRCs offer a tiered approach to the aging process, accommodating residents' changing needs. Upon entering, healthy adults can reside independently in single-family homes, apartments or condominiums. When assistance with everyday activities becomes necessary, they can move into assisted living or nursing care facilities. These communities give older adults the option to live in one location for the duration of their life, with much of their future care already figured out". (AARP-Family Caregiving Basics—About CCRCs)

When looking into CCRCs, you would ask a combination of the questions listed for assisted living and nursing homes.

PALLIATIVE CARE

"Palliative care" is specialized medical care for people living with a serious illness. This type of care is focused on relief from the symptoms and stress of a serious illness. The goal is to improve quality of life for both the patient and the family.

Palliative care is provided by a specially-trained team of doctors, nurses and other specialists who work together with a patient's other doctors to provide an extra layer of support. It is appropriate at any age and at **any stage in a serious illness, and it can be provided along with curative treatment.**" (GetPalliativeCare.org)

To find palliative care for home or onsite in hospital or SNF take a look at palliativecare.org. Again, find out the insurance and services they can offer in home or onsite. Always make sure you get your questions answered before making a determination.

HOSPICE CARE

During an illness that is terminal, you or your loved ones may talk with your doctor and decide the treatments meant to cure or slow a disease are no longer working, or you're ready to stop them. Your doctor can make a referral for hospice care, also known as end-of-life care.

You want relief from pain, shortness of breath, and other symptoms so that you can focus on the people and things you care about the most. That's when hospice, or end-of-life care, may help.

Hospice service simply focuses on the quality of your life instead of trying to cure a disease.

Your team may include a doctor, nurse, social worker, counselor, chaplain (if you are religious), home health aide, and trained volunteers. They work together to meet your physical, emotional, and spiritual needs.

Hospice is for family members, too. It offers counseling and help with practical things such as cleaning house and shopping." (Hospice WebMD)

Hospice can be provided in the home or in hospice beds (often located in hospitals and skilled nursing facilities). To qualify for hospice, generally the doctor has to indicate a prognosis of 6 months or less to live. However, if something changes you can come off hospice. Often it is heartbreaking for me to hear that a person was put on hospice and passed away two days later. Hospice can be a wonderful choice and allow pain relief and precious quality time. Don't feel as if you have to wait until the very end as your loved one may not receive the benefits of hospice in time.

As a caregiver you must investigate these services in regard to insurance and services available. A common concern is obtaining constant 24/7 home care (HHA or companion care) through hospice home care. Generally this is not the case (although there are always exceptions). Hospice will determine the amount of home care that is needed but you need to ask and be prepared to get additional help in the home as well.

Your Patient Advocate can assist you in locating hospice or palliative care services to suit your needs. You can find hospice near you at National Hospice and Palliative Care Organization (www.nhpco.org).

6

WHO PAYS FOR THIS/WHAT INSURANCE COVERS

Now that we have discussed hospitals, home care, skilling nursing care, nursing homes and the like—who pays for this care? This question is not easy to answer. There are different types of insurance, as well as paying out of pocket. It is of utmost importance to look into your insurance and what it covers not only for your current circumstances but to plan for the future. You can change your insurance at certain times (i.e. open enrollment periods, change of life, etc.) to better fit your needs. Do you remember Chapter 2? In your advanced planning you need to think about money or insurance that may be available to take care of your health needs. There are a few common concerns I want you to know about:

For those who have Medicare A—you must have 3-day inpatient hospital stay to receive insurance coverage for a skilled nursing facility. There is a difference between "observation and *admission." You have to be **admitted** to the hospital for 3 days to get insurance coverage for skilled nursing care after that hospital stay.*

NO basic insurance other than long-term care insurance currently pays for long-term home care. The only other exception currently is Community Medicaid in some states, such as New York.

Now I am not going to get into the nitty gritty details of insurance, but I will give you a very basic synopsis of some of the major ones and answer the questions I get asked most frequently:

MEDICARE

Medicare (www.medicare.gov) is the federal government program that provides health care coverage (health insurance) if you are 65+, under 65 and receiving Social Security Disability Insurance (SSDI) for a certain amount of time, or under 65 and with End-Stage Renal Disease (ESRD).

When you first enroll in Medicare and during certain times of the year, you can choose how you get your Medicare coverage. There are 2 main ways to get your Medicare coverage—Original Medicare (Part A and Part B) or a Medicare Advantage Plan (Part C). Some people need to get additional coverage, like Medicare prescription drug coverage or Medicare Supplement Insurance (Medigap).

PART A COVERS

- Inpatient care in a hospital
- Skilled nursing facility care
- Inpatient care in a skilled nursing facility (not custodial or long-term care)
- Hospice care
- Home health care (temporary)

PART B COVERS 2 TYPES OF SERVICES

- **Medically necessary services:** Services or supplies that are needed to diagnose or treat your medical condition and that meet accepted standards of medical practice.
- **Preventive services:** Health care to prevent illness (like the flu) or detect it at an early stage, when treatment is most likely to work best.

You pay nothing for most preventive services if you get the services from a health care provider who is approved by Medicare.

Part B covers things like:

- Clinical research
- Ambulance services

- Durable medical equipment (DME)
- Mental health
- Inpatient
- Outpatient
- Partial hospitalization
- Getting a second opinion before surgery
- Limited outpatient prescription drugs

Medigap is extra health insurance that you buy from a private company to pay health care costs not covered by Original Medicare, such as co-payments, deductibles, and health care if you travel outside the United States. Medigap policies don't cover long-term care, dental care, vision care, hearing aids, eyeglasses, and private-duty nursing. Most plans do not cover prescription drugs.

8 THINGS TO KNOW ABOUT MEDIGAP POLICIES

(www.medicare.gov)

1. You must have Medicare Part A and Part B.

2. A Medigap policy is different from a Medicare Advantage Plan. Those plans are ways to get Medicare benefits, while a Medigap policy only supplements your Original Medicare benefits.

. . .

3. You pay the private insurance company a monthly Premium for your Medigap policy. You pay this monthly premium in addition to the monthly Part B premium that you pay to Medicare.

4. A Medigap policy only covers one person. If you and your spouse both want Medigap coverage, you'll each have to buy separate policies.

5. You can buy a Medigap policy from any insurance company that's licensed in your state to sell one.

6. Any standardized Medigap policy is guaranteed renewable even if you have health problems. This means the insurance company can't cancel your Medigap policy as long as you pay the premium.

7. Some Medigap policies sold in the past cover prescription drugs. But, Medigap policies sold after January 1, 2006 aren't allowed to include prescription drug coverage. If you want prescription drug coverage, you can join a Medicare Prescription Drug Plan (Part D).

8. It's illegal for anyone to sell you a Medigap policy if you have

a Medicare Advantage Plan, unless you're switching back to Original Medicare.

Medicare Advantage Plans, sometimes called "Part C" or "MA Plans," are an "all in one" **alternative** to Original Medicare. They are offered by private companies approved by Medicare. If you join a Medicare Advantage Plan, you still have Medicare. These "bundled" plans include Medicare Part A (Hospital Insurance) and Medicare Part B (Medical Insurance), and usually Medicare prescription drug (Part D).

Medicare Advantage Plans cover all Medicare services. Some Medicare Advantage Plans also offer extra coverage, like vision, hearing and dental coverage.

THINGS TO KNOW ABOUT MEDICARE ADVANTAGE PLANS

1. You're still in the Medicare Program.

2. You still have Medicare rights and protections.

3. You still get complete Part A and Part B coverage through the plan. Some plans offer extra benefits that Original Medicare doesn't cover – like vision, hearing, or dental.

. . .

4. Your out-of-pocket costs may be lower in a Medicare Advantage plan. If so, this option may be more cost effective for you.

5. You can only join a plan at certain times during the year. In most cases, you're enrolled in a plan for a year.

6. You can join a Medicare Advantage Plan even if you have a pre-existing condition, except for End-Stage Renal Disease (ESRD).

7. You can check with the plan before you get a service to find out if it's covered and what your costs may be.

8. Following plan rules, like getting a referral to see a specialist in the plan's network, can keep your costs lower. Check with the plan.

9. Go to a doctor, other health care provider, facility, or supplier that belongs to the plan's network, so your services are covered and your costs are less. In most cases, this applies to Medicare Advantage HMOs and PPOs.

10. Providers can join or leave a plan's provider network

anytime during the year. Your plan can also change the providers in the network anytime during the year. If this happens, you may need to choose a new provider.

11. If you join a clinical research study, some costs may be covered by your plan. Call your plan for more information. Get your plan's contact information from a Personalized Search (under General Search), or search by plan name.

12. Medicare Advantage Plans can't charge more than Original Medicare for certain services like chemotherapy, dialysis, and skilled nursing facility care.

13. Medicare Advantage Plans have a yearly limit on your out-of-pocket costs for medical services. Once you reach this limit, you'll pay nothing for covered services. Each plan can have a different limit, and the limit can change each year. You should consider this when choosing a plan.

14. If the plan decides to stop participating in Medicare, you'll have to join another Medicare health plan or return to Original Medicare (www.medicare.gov). It is important to check if your current doctors or any medical facilities/services you may use take Medicare Advantage Plans before you decide.

MEDICAID (WWW.MEDICAID.GOV)

Medicaid provides health coverage to millions of Americans, including eligible low-income adults, children, pregnant women, elderly adults and people with disabilities. Medicaid is administered by states, according to federal requirements. The program is funded jointly by states and the federal government. Although the federal government pays a portion of the costs, Medicaid is administered and operated by states, and each state's program is a little different depending on the needs and goals of that state.

Since Medicaid is administered by the Medicaid agency in your state, eligibility may vary from one state to another. In New York, and perhaps other states, make sure you investigate whether Medicaid can assist in your long-term care goals. Speak to your Elder Lawyer, Special Needs Attorney, and Patient Advocate/Care Coordinator.

LONG TERM CARE INSURANCE

Unlike traditional health insurance, long-term care is designed to cover long-term services and supports, including personal and custodial care (also called personal care). Non-skilled service or care includes help with bathing, dressing, eating, getting in and out of bed or chair, moving around, and using the bathroom in a variety of settings such as your home, a community organization, or other facility.

Long-term care insurance policies reimburse policyholders a

daily amount (up to a pre-selected limit) for services to assist them with activities of daily living such as:

Bathing—Washing oneself by sponge bath or in the bathtub or shower.

Dressing—Putting on and taking off all items of clothing and any necessary braces, fasteners, or artificial limbs.

Eating—Feeding oneself by getting food into the body from a receptacle or by a feeding tube or intravenously.

Continence—The ability to maintain control of bowel and bladder functions.

Toileting—Getting to and from the toilet, getting on and off the toilet and performing associated personal hygiene functions.

Transferring—Moving into and out of a bed, chair or wheelchair.

You can select a range of care options and benefits. A monetary sum is generally paid by an insurance company to a recipient or to a care provider for services that the insurance policy covers.

The cost of your policy is based on things like:

- How old you are when you buy the policy
- The maximum amount that a policy will pay per day
- The maximum number of days (years) that a policy will pay
- The maximum amount per day times the number of

days determines the lifetime maximum amount that the policy will pay
- Any optional benefits you choose, such as benefits that increase with inflation

If you are in poor health, you may not qualify for long-term care insurance as most individual policies require medical underwriting. In some cases, you may be able to buy a limited amount of coverage, or coverage at a higher "non-standard" rate. Some group policies do not require underwriting.

Many long-term care insurance policies have **limits on how long or how much they will pay**. Some policies will pay the costs of your long-term care for two to five years, while other insurance companies offer policies that will pay your long-term care costs **for as long as you live**—no matter how much it costs. But there are very few that have no such limits.

Before you buy a policy, be aware that the insurance company may raise the premium on your policy. It is a good idea to request information on the company's premium rate history.

https://longtermcare.acl.gov/costs-how-to-pay/what-is-long-term-care-insurance/

SOCIAL SECURITY DISABILITY (WWW.SSA.GOV)

Social Security pays benefits to people who can't work because they have a medical condition that's expected to last at least one year or result in death. Federal law requires this very strict definition of disability. Certain family members of disabled workers can also receive money from Social Security. This is NOT partial disability or short-term disability.

TAKE-AWAYS

1. Learn now what your insurance covers.

2. Call your insurance company before you pick a doctor or have a planned medical procedure to get information on what will be covered.

3. Plan ahead and do your homework before you change your insurance. If you are wondering whether Medicare is best for you, do your homework (or contact your Patient Advocate for assistance) to see what works for you and your medical condition, medications, doctors, and budget.

4. When planning long term it may be helpful to speak with a Financial Advisor as well as a long term care insurance provider to determine what options may be right for you.

7

AN OUNCE OF PREVENTION IS WORTH A POUND OF CURE

Here are some **Adult Preventive Services that experts suggest you speak with your doctor/clinician about.**

This is not an exhaustive list. This is a guideline, and perhaps you may want to add it to your notebook of questions to ask your clinician. New insights are discovered often in the health care world. It can be hard to keep up with them, but asking the questions can help your clinician bring you the latest insights.

PREVENTIVE SERVICES

Free preventive care: Many insurance plans provide these services at no cost, without charging co-pays or deductible payments.

. . .

Talk to Your Doctor about Abdominal Aortic Aneurysm

If you have ever smoked, talk with your doctor about abdominal aortic aneurysm (AAA).

Recommended especially for: Men aged 65-75 who have ever smoked tobacco.

Talk with a Doctor about Your Alcohol Use

If you are concerned about your drinking, ask your doctor about screening and counseling.

Recommended for: Adults

Talk with Your Doctor about Taking Aspirin Every Day

Talk to your doctor about taking an aspirin every day to help lower your risk of heart attack or stroke.

Recommended for: Men aged 45-79 and women aged 55-79.

Get Your Blood Pressure Checked

Get your blood pressure checked at least once every 1-2 years. Ask your doctor how often you need to get it checked.

Recommended for: Adults

Get Your Cholesterol Checked

Get your cholesterol checked once every 5 years.

Recommended for: Men aged 35 and older, and men and women at high risk, aged 20 and older.

Get Tested for Colorectal Cancer

Talk with your doctor about options for getting tested.

Recommended for: Adults aged 50-75.

Note: For people at average risk for colorectal cancer, the **American Cancer Society** recommends starting regular screening at **age 45**. This can be done either with a sensitive test that looks for signs of cancer in a person's stool (a stool-based test), or with an exam that looks at the colon and rectum (a visual exam). Talk to your health care provider about which tests might be good options for you, and to your insurance provider about your coverage. No matter which test you choose, the most important thing is to get screened.

Get Tested for Chlamydia, Gonorrhea, and Syphilis

Talk with your doctor to find out if you need to be tested for chlamydia, gonorrhea, or syphilis.

Recommended for: Adults who have had sex or are at high risk.

Talk with Your Doctor about Depression

Talk with your doctor about how you are feeling if you have been sad, down, or hopeless.

Recommended for: Adults

Take Steps to Prevent Type 2 Diabetes

If you have high blood pressure, ask your doctor if you need to be screened for type 2 diabetes.

Recommended for: Adults with high blood pressure.

Get Help with Healthy Eating

If your doctor has told you that you are at risk for heart disease or diabetes, ask about dietary counseling.

Recommended for: Adults with high cholesterol or at risk for heart disease or diabetes.

Talk to Your Doctor about Preventing Falls

If you are worried about falls, ask how exercise, physical therapy, and vitamin D supplements might help you prevent falls.

Recommended for: Adults over 65.

. . .

Get Tested for Hepatitis C

Get tested for hepatitis C at least one time if you were born between 1945 and 1965.

Recommended for: Adults born between 1945 and 1965.

Get Tested for HIV

Get tested for HIV at least once. You may need to get tested more often depending on your risk.

Recommended for: Adults

Get Screened for Lung Cancer

Ask the doctor about screening for lung cancer if you have a history of heavy smoking and you smoke now or have quit within the past 15 years. An example of heavy smoking is smoking 1 pack of cigarettes a day for 30 years—or 2 packs a day for 15 years.

Recommended for: Adults aged 55-80 who have smoked heavily.

Watch Your Weight

Ask your doctor if you are at a healthy weight.

Recommended for: Adults

Talk to the Doctor about Skin Cancer

If you have fair (pale) skin, talk to the doctor about how to reduce your risk of skin cancer.

Recommended for: Adults under 24 years old with fair skin.

Get Help to Quit Tobacco

If you use tobacco, ask your doctor about services to help you quit.

Recommended for: Adults who use tobacco.

Prostate Cancer Screening-Men

The American Cancer Society (ACS) recommends: men make an informed decision with a health care provider about whether to be tested for prostate cancer. Research has not yet proven that the potential benefits of testing outweigh the harms of testing and treatment. ACS believes that men should not be tested without first learning about what we know and don't know about the risks and possible benefits of testing and treatment.

Starting at age 50, men should talk to a health care provider about the pros and cons of testing so they can decide if testing is the right choice for them.

If you are African-American or have a father or brother who

had prostate cancer before age 65, you should have this talk with a health care provider starting at age 45.

If you decide to be tested, you should get a PSA blood test with or without a rectal exam. How often you're tested will depend on your PSA level.

Get a Pneumonia Vaccine

Ask your doctor for a pneumonia vaccine.

Recommended for: Adults over 65 and others at high risk.

Get a Seasonal Flu Vaccine

Get a flu vaccine every year to protect yourself and others from the flu.

Recommended for: Adults

Tdap

Protect from tetanus, diphtheria, and whooping cough (pertussis). Everyone needs to get the Tdap shot once, and pregnant women need a dose during every pregnancy.

After you get a Tdap shot, get a TD shot every 10 years to keep you protected from tetanus and diphtheria.

. . .

Shingles Prevention

If you're age 50 or older: Get shots to prevent shingles. Shingles causes a painful rash that can last for months.

If you're age 65 or older: Ask your doctor, nurse, or pharmacist about other shots you may need to stay healthy.

PREVENTIVE CARE FOR WOMEN

Free preventive care: Many insurance plans provide these services at no cost, without charging co-pays or deductible payments.

Get Your Well-Woman Visit Every Year

See a doctor or nurse for a checkup once a year.

Recommended for: Women under 65.

Choose the Right Birth Control

If you are interested in birth control, talk with a doctor about your options.

Get a Bone Density Test

Get your bone density tested starting at age 65.

Recommended for: Women over 65, and younger women at high risk for osteoporosis.

Get Tested for Breast Cancer

Get a mammogram every 2 years.

Recommended for: Women aged 50-74

Note: The American Cancer Society states:

• **Women of ages 40 to 44** should have the choice to start annual breast cancer screening with mammograms (x-rays of the breast) if they wish to do so.

• **Women of ages 45 to 54** should get mammograms every year.

• **Women 55 and older** should switch to mammograms every 2 years, or can continue yearly screening.

• Screening should continue as long as a woman is in good health and is expected to live 10 more years or longer.

• **All women** should be familiar with the known benefits, limitations, and potential harms linked to breast cancer screening.

Get Tested for Cervical Cancer

Get a Pap test every 3 years. If you are age 30 or older and get a

Pap test and an HPV test, you can get screened every 5 years instead.

Recommended for: Women aged 21-65

Get Enough Folic Acid

Recommended for: Women who could become pregnant.

Take Steps to Protect Yourself from Relationship Violence

If you think your partner might be abusive, talk with your doctor about getting help.

The recommendations on prevention and vaccines come directly from the *U.S. Preventive Services Task Force (USPSTF, the Advisory Committee on Immunization Practices (ACIP), the Bright Futures (BF) Guidelines,* and the *Institute of Medicine's (IOM) Committee on Preventive Services for Women* unless otherwise noted to be from the American Cancer Society.

So now you have some idea of the tests all of us should consider to remain healthy. What else is there for you as the caregiver or your loved one? In all of this remarkable caregiving you provide, you **must** also take care of yourself. Caregiving is difficult and it's generally for the long hall. I recommend the following:

It takes a village—ASK for help from family, neighbors, friends, follow congregants from your place of worship, etc. Make a list of things like meal preparation, school pick up, check-ins, laundry, visits, transportation and all the other things that would help your life or the life of the person you are caring for easier. You will be amazed how people will react when you ask them to do a concrete task. Often people want to help but don't know how.

Find a support group—Caregiving can feel very isolating. Seek out support groups either in person or online. There are group for those providing care for others with the same diagnosis, as well as general support groups. Just knowing there are others out there coping with similar issues can be comforting. In addition, they can provide practical advice.

Take time for yourself—You may feel like that's impossible but it's not—and it IS necessary. Find things that give you joy. That may mean something like taking a walk, taking time to socialize with friends, meditation, a vacation, a phone call with a friend or something altogether different, but you must do it. You must fill your own pitcher before you can fill someone else's and clearly you have a lot of pitchers to fill.

Utilize therapies—There has been more emphasis in the medical community on non-traditional therapies/modalities.

Pain management may utilize chiropractic, acupuncture, massage or aroma therapy. There is also use of important modules like music, art, equine, pet, and drama therapy demonstrating impact not only in quality of life for patient and caregivers but easing of symptoms. So do your research (get a Patient Advocate) and be open to ideas that may help.

Hire a Patient Advocate—The right Patient Advocate and Care Coordinator can assist not only with the navigation of the health care and everything we have discussed in this book, but also help find the support groups, setting up list of tasks for your "village" to assist and be your sounding board.

8

WHAT'S NEXT—IT'S TRUE YOU NEED PATIENT ADVOCACY AND CARE COORDINATION

S o, my dear superheroes, I have thrown a lot of information your way. It is a lot for a healthy person to get these things straight never-the-less for a patient or a caregiver. You may be thinking *"the last thing I needed was more to do."* You may now feel empowered with information but still overwhelmed, frustrated and tired.

Here is what you need to do:

- Keep care and health a priority
- Keep copious notes
- Contact those who can best help, and
- Speak with a private Patient Advocate

HOW TO FIND A PATIENT ADVOCATE?

Contact Care Answered at careanswered.com or call us 516-584-2007

Contact your employer and say: "Is there any way you can provide a much-needed benefit to myself and my colleagues and hire a Patient Advocate to help us navigate through the health-care system for ourselves and our loved ones?" Remember you are not alone in this request. The cost of caregiving in the United States costs businesses $36 Billion annually. Then give them CareAnswered.com and our phone number. We can discuss ways of having a Patient Advocate added as one of your work benefits or set up an "Ask the Patient Advocate" lunch.

Advoconnection.com is another resource. You can input your needs and your zip code to find a Patient Advocate near you.

Not all Patient Advocates are created equal and not all focus on the same issues. So here are some questions that are important to ask to get the right fit. You will find a Health Notebook at the back of this book where you can record your answers.

After describing your situation, ask, "Have you dealt with similar situations?"

Why?—Patient Advocates have different specialties. Generally experience with a particular kind of advocacy and care coordination will provide a comfort level for you. However, if they have not dealt with the particular issue, it does not automatically mean they are not the right advocate for you. You should ask what they have dealt with that may be similar.

Are you a Board Certified Patient Advocate (BCPA)?

Why?—Because it states they have Patient Advocacy Certification. Just like with any field, it means they passed the test. Having this Certification demonstrates that the Patient Advocate possesses relevant advocacy expertise, including an understanding of best practices and standards. In addition, it means they understand the ethics for patient advocacy, which is a must. The credentials to pass the test also includes empowerment, right and equity, healthcare access, finance and management, medical knowledge and the healthcare system.

Are you/ your business insured?

Why?—Because businesses that are insured have taken the necessary precautions to protect themselves and you which adds to their legitimacy, confidence, seriousness, and competency.

How many years have you been an advocate and what was your experience prior to being an advocate?

Why?—This gives you a feel for the advocate's level of experience, but perhaps more importantly, it lets you learn a bit more about them. This is for the care of yourself or your loved one; you want someone with whom you feel comfortable.

What is the cost of services

Why?—There will likely be a cost. You want to make sure you can afford to pay for their services, of course. And in all things, you get what we pay for (this excludes those fabulous non-profit advocacy groups out there that can provide some assistance free or at a low cost). If you find a great Patient Advocate, don't let cost necessarily stand in your way. Ask if there is a payment plan or something that could make payments easier for you. The sooner a Patient Advocate is involved the better the potential outcome, including reduction of your stress and frustrations.

Do you have the ability to take on a new client with the kind of needs I described right now?

Why?—You want to make sure they have the time and ability to take on you/your loved one as the client. If they can't and you can wait, ask them when/if they think they will be able to. You don't want a Patient Advocate who is going on vacation or too busy at the time you need services.

Will you personally be my/ my loved one's patient advocate?

Why?—There is nothing wrong if that answer is no or we won't know who will be assigned to you until after you are officially working with us. But I believe it's good to know from the start. It's like when a contractor comes to you home and gives you an estimate for work in your home and then you never see that person again. It's only annoying when you assumed that person would be on the job site or you made the decision based on the contractor's experience. So always ask.

Once you have hired your Patient Advocate, you will still be a superhero; but hopefully you can breathe easier and your cape will be a little straighter and maybe even ironed.

HEALTH NOTEBOOK

Ask Questions at the clinician's office, such as:

What is the test for?

How many times have you done this procedure?

When will I get the results?

Why do I need this treatment?

Are there any alternatives?

What are the possible complications?

Which hospital is best for my needs? (Which hospital has the least infection rate?)

How do you spell the name of that drug?

Are there any side effects?

Will this medicine interact with medicines that I'm already taking?

Is there anything the doctor said that you did not fully understand? If so, ASK NOW. By reiterating what the doctor says both s/he and you will know if you truly understood. At the very least please ask the ASK ME 3 (National Safety Foundation) questions:

What is my main problem?

What do I need to do?

Why is it important to me?

Notes

Tips and questions to ask when looking into Home Health Aides or Companion Care:

1. Include your loved ones and primary care physician in the discussion about the need for home care and the type of care needed.

----

2. Make a list of daily activities in which you/your loved one may need assistance.

----

3. Determine what hours of the day and how many days a week you/your loved one needs care.

----

4. Prepare a list of medications (include supplements) that include when the medications are taken and what each medication is taken for. Keep in mind many home care agencies can't

have their aides "administer" medications. This means they cannot take the medicines out of the bottle to give you but they can give reminders. (Always ask any care provider what they are able to do based on your list of daily activities in tip 2.)

----

5. Make a list of personality traits you/your loved one would find ideal—remember this person is in your home. Some examples: preference for someone chatty or quiet/reserved, is there a language in which you are more comfortable communicating, is there a preferred gender, is there a culture that you feel most comfortable around?

----

6. If you decide to find a home care agency or choose a home care provider privately, make sure a background check is done.
☐

----

7. If possible, interview all perspective home care providers. Sometimes it is not possible to interview them in person or on the phone, so tips 1-6 are even more important to provide to the homecare provider.

---

8. Have a loved one or Patient Advocate stop by unannounced to make sure the homecare provider is meeting expectations. ☐

Notes

Tips and questions to ask when looking for SNF short-term rehab:

1. Visit potential sites and take note of smell, activity, interaction between patients and between staff and patients.

----

2. How many days do they offer each type of rehab (Physical Therapy (PT), Occupational Therapy (OT), and Speech Therapy)?

----

3. Obtain a list of medication from the hospital or home. Ask if the SNF is going to be able to access these medications so they will be available at upon arrival. This is especially important for prescriptions that are unusual or expensive or being used off-label (medication prescribed "off-label" is when a doctor prescribes medication that has been approved for different conditions than the condition being treated).

----

4. If your loved one is a fall risk, what precautions does the facility take to avoid falls?

----

5. What are visiting hours?

----

6. If your loved one has a condition that will impact their ability to be effective at rehab (i.e. pain, confusion, dizziness that may make it more challenging for them to cooperate with movement needed for therapy) make sure this is being treated at the hospital before they leave for rehab. Also bring it to the attention of the rehab facility immediately and ask if they have a specialist who can simultaneously treat it if needed.

----

7. If there are other medical concerns, make sure they have the equipment and personnel necessary (i.e. ventilator or dialysis) to treat that condition.

----

8. Review the PRI (Patient Review Instrument) to make sure it has accurate information, as this is what is sent to the potential rehabilitation sites. If something seems inaccurate, alert the nurse and ask them to make corrections before it is sent out. ☐

----

9. Hire a Patient Advocate before hospital discharge so that you can be the loved one. Patient Advocates can utilize their experience and make this process easier for you and you can have peace of mind. ☐

----

10. You want to articulate your loved ones baseline to the social worker, nurse and staff at the short-term rehab. "Baseline" means their skill level before entering the hospital that led to the need for rehab. Example is your loved one fell and broke their leg. Before they broke their leg they used a cane to walk. Therefore the baseline is they walked with a cane. So that would be the goal for rehab (barring any other circumstance).

----

11. Ask immediately when the care plan can be scheduled. The meeting brings all staff together (Social Worker, Nurse, PT, OT, Recreation, Speech etc. to discuss progress and next steps. The caregiver and patient are crucial in this plan. A Patient Advocate can represent the family/patient or join them in this meeting. They will make sure the care plan is clear and the steps toward reaching at least the baseline are clear to all. ☐

Notes

Questions when selecting a Private Patient Advocate:

After describing your situation, ask, "Have you dealt with similar situations?"

_____

_____

_____

Are you a Board Certified Patient Advocate (BCPA)?

_____

_____

_____

Are you/ your business insured?

_____

_____

_____

How many years have you been an advocate and what was your experience prior to being an advocate?

_____

_____

_____

What is the cost of services?

_____

_____

_____

Do you have the ability to take on a new client with the kind of needs I described right now?

_____

_____

_____

Will you personally be my/my loved one's Patient Advocate?

_____

_____

_____

Notes

_____

_____

_____

_____

_____

_____

Tips and questions to ask when looking into assisted living:

What is the staff-to-resident ratio? (which staff is included in this ratio i.e. CNA, Nurses)

Do you have a designated (sometimes referred to as memory units) area of living for those struggling with dementia?

How often is a psychiatrist available to memory unit residents?

My loved one has dementia and I know there are many different stages and changes that can occur. Do you have experience with residents who get agitated? I know every resident can be different but can you give me an example of some practices you may employ?

What is the protocol for medication administration? Is it given within an hour for example or is it exactly on time?

How is the efficacy of medication monitored? (i.e. if a resident comes in for their usual medication but is unusually lethargic or agitated is there a protocol that takes place?)

What activities do you have for residents and how do you assist in the engagement of these activities?

How do you engage residents in activities when they are non-verbal? (Especially important if your loved one has dementia)

What activities are offered?

Do you allow outside and/or companion aides or Home Health Aide (HHA)? Keep in mind this will be an additional cost.

If we run out of money to pay for this assisted living, is there any way to stay here? If not, do you help us find appropriate placement?

If one becomes less ambulatory (i.e. needs a walker or wheel-chair to get around) will they be able to stay here?

Tips and questions to ask when looking into Home Health Aides or Companion Care:

1. Include your loved ones and primary care physician in the discussion about the need for home care and the type of care needed.

----

2. Make a list of daily activities in which you/your loved one may need assistance.

----

3. Determine what hours of the day and how many days a week you/your loved one needs care.

----

4. Prepare a list of medications (include supplements) that includes when the medications are taken and what each medication is taken for. You will find a medication list at the back of the book. Keep in mind many home care agencies can't

have their aides "administer" medications. This means they cannot take the medication out of the bottle to give to the patient, but they can give reminders. (Always ask any Care Provider what they are able to do based on your list of daily activities in tip 2.)

----

5. Make a list of personality traits you/your loved one would find ideal—remember this person is in your home. Some examples: preference for someone chatty or quiet/reserved, is there a language in which you are more comfortable communicating, is there a preferred gender, is there a culture that you feel most comfortable around?

----

6. If you decide to find a home care agency or choose a home care provider privately, make sure a background check is done.

----

7. If possible, interview all perspective home care providers.

Sometimes it is not possible to interview them in person or on the phone, so tips 1-6 are even more important to provide to the homecare provider. Notes for interview:

----

8. Have a loved one or Patient Advocate stop by unannounced to make sure the homecare provider is meeting expectations.

Notes

Notes

Notes

Care
Answered

Name

Date

Current Medicines (including prescribed, OTC, herbal...)

Medication	Dosage and Instruction	Reason	Comments: (ie- who prescribed, time of day taken, affects of usage, food combinations,etc.)

Name

Date

Care
Answered

Current Medicines (including prescribed, OTC, herbal...)

Medication	Dosage and Instruction	Reason	Comments: (ie- who prescribed, time of day taken, affects of usage, food combinations,etc.)

ABOUT THE AUTHOR

Nicole Christensen, MS, BCPA is a professional Patient Advocate and CEO of Care Answered, a NY based healthcare coordination and patient advocacy organization specializing in health transitions for adults and their families. Her professional advocacy experience began in 1997 in Washington DC as an advocate for senior citizens.

In her career even before launching Care Answered in 2014, she had the opportunity to develop and strengthen advocacy programs in Washington DC, NYC and Long Island.

Nicole is the mother of 2 amazing boys and the youngest of 6 children. Caregiving and Advocacy is in her DNA. She began Care Answered because of her knowledge: It is often absolutely overwhelming and paralyzing when trying to access needed care for those you love. Care Answered was developed as a solution; advocating for one's best care and giving caregivers peace of mind.

Made in the USA
Monee, IL
27 January 2020

20961473R00075